Keep All the Parts

Roy Young

Five Leaves Publications

For M and her sponsorship of the arts, M, H, & J
and for my walking companion, T.

Contents

Keep All the Parts
Roy Young

Published in 2024 by Five Leaves Publications
14a Long Row, Nottingham NG1 2DH
www.fiveleaves.co.uk
www.fiveleavesbookshop. co.uk

ISBN: 978-1-915434-13-5

Printed in Great Britain

if pieces you take something to
keep you the need to parts all

if something to pieces you take
parts all you keep to the need

if you take pieces to something
keep the parts all you need to

if you take something to pieces
you need to keep all the parts

For this moment

time has no forwards
or backwards,
as the river holds
the evening light
in her current.

Stillness caught in motion.
Waterfowl pause
on the flooded scrape,
we stand where
the chain ferry crossed,

in one frame of a movie
on the beauty of ordinary,
a confluence
where many have stood

at evening,
in a sequence of evenings.

Tree span

trees bridge space

between river bend
               and sky—

fingering wind's fluidity

and the push   and pull

of water
      against
         the currents
             of the day

they hold us for a   breath

strong against the curve of land

to inspect colours
feel the hue   and tone
of blue

     suspended

in green
and rose grey

branches grip the   betweenness
of things

as once our shadows
pass briefly

            as clouds do

Map of you

I have made a map of you,
just in case I need to retrace
the contours of your touch,
and feel again your landscape,
of saddleback swales and peaks,
where I have willingly been lost.

I have made a map of you,
just in case I need to survey
the scars and crags of absence,
to feel again your sense of place
in woods and meadows
where I have been safely held.

I have made a map of you
just in case I need to locate
waking with you,
to see a sun-chiselled skyline
of scarp and dip slope,
where I have found home ground.

I have made a map of you
just in case
a poem is not enough.

Solstice

No need to let the past
hijack this day's end,
it is enough on its own
with house martins
blessing the last
of the evening's spaces
with *cries-here* and *cries-there*.

Now bats with pendulum flicks
cloaked in black and turquoise
sing a hymn silently for us.
They know how to worship seasons,
the moving of sun to farthest west,
and how to go and come again
in precise evening rituals,
older than ours.

Ice beast

The glacier left its dirty finger-
print in this u-shaped valley,
arching moraines thrown up
by push and shove of grimy snout.

The beast stood here once,
screaming defiance with gushing
flared nostrils, crevasses mouthing
and grinding rock to powder.

Now the beast has fled.
Chased up the mountain by our fires,
shrunken, skulking in a cirque
between the naked peaks.

The old caldron useless without
snow to pack and freeze,
to squeeze, chisel and gouge
a landscape with icy threat.

Hunger stones

We should write
on these stones,
like our ancestors did:
If you read me, weep,
the river is dry
famine is close.

We should write
on these stones
like our ancestors did:
Stay above this place
tsunami cannot claw you back
and swallow children.

We should write
on these stones
like our ancestors did:
Flood reached here,
made fields sudden seas,
drowned all hope.

We should write something
on these stones,
say to ancestors:
we took note
but preferred to gamble
with loaded dice.

Planning permission

History sticks to some places, stops change, but not here.

Here is a place where anyone who passes can think of it as new—to be worked, used for profit. Yesterday, indeed all the yesterdays that shaped *Here* don't really count; have no voice. *Now* is the only time that matters in these places that slip into the future, without the burden of too much past. Old people in the village recall a past, and the stories older people told them. But mostly things are forgotten or were misunderstood anyway. Hindsight should not be mistaken for wisdom. *Here* is a place where history settles like leaves, fragments and is buried in unmarked graves. *Here* is an everyday, ordinary landscape.

So yes, go ahead: cut trees, dig, move, drain the fields. Wipe the valley landscape clean of its past, the forgotten things that sustained it. *Here* is a stranger we do not know enough about to care if they come, or go. The future will be dealt with by others.

in the valley now
buzzards circle, and see us
blindly walk away

The assassin

chooses her rooftop wisely
            clear sight lines
            cover behind
and from her vantage point
inspects the killing ground
the zone of river and lanes
an arena of buildings and park

she—a wanderer
a pilgrim in this city
breeding violence
she knows how hearts beat
and how they are stopped

dead

she watches
for the weak and unsuspecting

slips the ledge

stoops

strikes

Fully organic

Our decomposers are always
ready to pounce
on a fallen leaf
or body
to rapidly release
carbon from its bonds
in an orgy of
biological digestion.

Whether you are waste
or something you think
more useful—

we can recycle here.

Forest engineers

Acorns have ideas
of trees in them
and dreams of forest
if they can tempt
a passing jay to un-cup
an autumn promise
store it in the forgetfulness
of bramble and thorn
and wait for the taste
of spring seed leaves
and the green of wilding.

The Guardian, June 2021:

"More than half the trees in two new woodlands in lowland England have been planted
not by landowners, charities or machines but by jays…. during 'passive rewilding',
thrushes spread seeds of bramble, blackthorn and hawthorn, and this scrub then
provided natural thorny tree 'guards' for oaks…"

Sequoia sempervierens

On the slopes above the Severn
a tribe of giant Coast Redwoods
stand strong along Offa's Dyke.

These trees know power of place,
how dynasties persist
and how to hold up a sky.

They pan gold from sunlight,
as it flows across velvet-deep
burnt sienna forest floor.

An experiment in forestry
unlocks and stores time
where myths and histories

grow between columns.
Our smallness is held steady
beneath a perfumed cloud-canopy.

Charles Ackers Redwood Grove and Naylor Pinetum at Leighton, Wales, contains one
of the most famous and historically significant stands of trees in the UK.

What trees do

The copse at the crossroads
fills the air
                        a symphony
            swirling
                                    roaring
this is how trees compose.

The copse at the crossroads
smells of earth
                        an army
            shoulder to shoulder
                                    dug-in
this is how trees conquer.

The copse at the crossroads
holds the sky
                        a cathedral
            buttressed
                                    enfolding
this is how trees bless.

I paint the copse in winter
                        and in spring,
I try to paint what trees do.

Then summer comes
                        and in autumn
they are gone.

I see what trees do.

They mark time.

Erosion

Slow folded Jurassic cliffs
eaten by a predatory sea,
with the suck and gnaw
of wave and tide.
Traces of old life scatter,
frozen time dissolves.
Sediment encases
sea cucumber,
bladderwrack,
cling and kiss of mussels—
the traces of a day
nobody may ever know.

Extinction stories

You don't have to die with your hypothesis,
unless you're a dinosaur
not fully cognisant of astronomy
and the possibilities of meteorites.

You don't have to decline and fall,
unless you're an auroch,
unfamiliar with the Roman arena
and the way the odds are stacked.

You don't have to perish with your plan
unless you're a dodo,
not paying attention to the possibility of flight
and the beauties of wind and air.

You don't have to succumb to your theory,
unless you're a whale,
with no grounding in the classics
and the fate of Moby Dick.

You don't have to abandon the future
unless you're a buffalo,
untutored in the principles of ballistics
on the open plains without cover.

You don't have to give up on survival
unless you're an orangutang,
not briefed on forest fragmentation,
and us apes, who want your space.

Ocean song

The language of whales is deep and long,
they see and feel the world with sound,
these gentle keepers of ocean song.

Their calls, complex, loud and strong,
chart routes with echo's sure rebound.
The language of whales is deep and long.

They seek out where krill might throng,
where safe birthing waters still abound,
these gentle keepers of ocean song.

Pods know sadness when one is gone,
and sing loud when one is found,
the language of whales is deep and long.

They feel danger, they see wrong,
they flee from the hunters who surround,
these gentle keepers of ocean song.

Their whispered story is beyond
our understanding of nature's sound.
The language of whales is deep and long.
These gentle keepers of ocean song.

Sea level

greedy sea
gnawing at rocks
swilling sand
between stumps
old teeth blunted

days do not matter
only wave time
she has learned tricks
of wreckers
of luring
of melting ice
of dissolving
evidence of things
once here

don't mistake
calm for love
she is a beast
waiting

she beckons us
closer
closer
until we hear
her whisper
as we drown

Dance forms

a pair of swans draw
intersecting parabolas
across Holme Pit

spring slowly unveiling
certainty as a Sarabande
with circle and bow

four cygnets
come to spoil
the symmetry

spring celebrating
its promise as a Gigue
of dart and fold

today one cygnet
plays out loneliness
a Pavane

spring is relentless in its rhythm
of expectance and loss

Notes on a heron

1.

question mark by river
asks for calm to pluck life
from the mirror of morning

2.

lonely in stillness
of stare and search
a hunter halting time

3.

patience a deadly weapon
wrapped in tall
sleek silence

4.

surprise familiar places
with sudden flight
from grey to gone

5.

distant call and coldness
freezes reflected
image of absence

Maybe

the weeds are out of lockdown.
Spring said go, and they did.

You left the raised beds in winter
with a brown frown

now they have a green smile.
On your knees and pray

clear the ground for a good harvest,
or any kind of harvest at all.

This is not a special place
but people made it through before.

They had their robin on a spade
and a blackbird with a worm.

Maybe you can make it too.

Midsummer dream

the low evening sun
ignites flower heads
the garden enfolds us
high grasses bask
in the transience of swallows
and the whisper of things not fixed
but fragile in their keeping

work done and tools aside
we run our fingers along
the ways we are part of a place
and know how it shelters
warm fragments
fast bats and
slow insects

for a while

in a dusk
a song thrush
thinks
is opera

Taking stock

the secret's out
summers over—

the swallows know it
by their going

in the folds of tired leaves
hedgerows practice alchemy

blackbirds raid
tiny grapes by the door

windfall thuds mark time
in the orchard

I taste the last of the season
on the raspberry abacus

calculate the number
of seasons that perhaps remain

Not in my back yard

The fox pauses
before the ditch
turns its head,

the old tree
with elbows in the frost
watches,

a black SUV noses the hedgerow
wheels rutting the meadow,
a new beast from somewhere
sniffing and scraping
at the morning.

Insulated
beneath the car carapace
developers eye the opportunity
purr and lazy growl
to the satisfied hum
of aircon:

farming is finished
on these edge lands;
fragment nature
and it's easy to take;
push the countryside
out of town
as far as it will go;
space is money
and trees look better
in a brochure
on a skyline
or a guided walk
with signs to say
bluebells are bluebells;

plan a sustainable
urban extension
with affordable houses
retail hubs
and sheds for storing
of stuff delivered
just in time;

we will paint
the warehouses blue
to show environmental concern
as we build our way
out of problems;

these are just nibbles at nature,
at the edge of nothing special
like anybody's future.

the beast
moves on
as beasts do

leaving the morning
in the field

for now.

Something doesn't add up

Add, subtract, multiply and divide,
modellers divine our chaotic lives.
They distinguish science fiction
from science fact, clarify
assumptions, and with cool calculus
map our future, how we should act.

So, don't ask where freedom sits
in algebra with known unknowns,
random coefficients, and no terms
for bloody-mindedness. Don't ask
about angles in our geometry
of fuzzy lines and dots not joining,

or the need to see a lover, walk on a hill,
or say goodbye. Just hope the sums are right.

Charge sheet

For rainforests,
       whose complexity
       we answer
       with ruthless fire.

For coral reefs,
       with colours so blinding
       we need to bleach
       the living rock.

For grasslands,
       whose green sea
       we reclaim
       and overwork.

For oceans,
       where dolphins whisper
       your plastic
       is all around.

For deserts,
       whose emptiness
       we spread
       by neglect.

For tundra,
       whose simplicity
       we squander
       with pipes and flares.

For small islands,
       whose innocence
       we drown
       in a creeping sea.

For mountains and hills,
       whose silence
       we log
       and terrace.

For wetlands,
>whose bounty
>we drain
>and shrink.

For icecaps and glaciers,
>whose blue indifference
>we force
>to retreat.

For everyday landscapes,
>whose ugliness
>we construct
>and accept.

For a biosphere,
>whose oneness
>we forget.

Repair bill

you can't mend silence
fix loss or

absences so large
excuses cannot fill

so no talk of healing
words hide neglect

no pardon
can be asked

make do now with
torn land and seascapes

hope green or
blue will mend

remind us
nature is finite

and of itself

Summer's end

gestures of departure
across the tired autumn meadow
cut baled and cleared

insects fewer now
caught in last
graceful swoops
and turns of swallows
who spread the itch of leaving
along telephone wires

the old know what struggle is
the young must find
the meaning of distance
and return

Gaia's song

May we understand with forest,
and smell the power of green.

May we know with oceans,
and hear the sounds of blue.

May we search with mountains,
and see the edge of cloudscapes.

May we walk with grasslands,
and taste the shape of wind.

May we rest with water,
and touch a dream of smooth.

May we touch ice and need it.
May we feel heat and read it.
May we see change and heed it.

Five Leaves New Poetry

Five Leaves presents a new series of debut poetry pamphlets by East Midlands writers, showcasing the exciting emerging talent from our region.

All pamphlets can be ordered from our websites.

Five Leaves Bookshop/Publications
14a Long Row, Nottingham NG1 2DH
bookshop@fiveleaves.co.uk   **0115 837 3097**
www.fiveleaves.co.uk   www.fiveleavesbookshop.co.uk